Linck & Mülhahn

Ruby Thomas is an actor and writer born in London. She wrote a piece for the Royal Court Theatre's *Living Newspaper* (2020), and her plays *Either* (2019) and *The Animal Kingdom* (2022) were both first performed at the Hampstead Theatre. *Linck & Mülhahn* was shortlisted for the George Devine Award 2022.

T0333842

RUBY THOMAS

Linck & Mülhahn

faber

First published in 2023
by Faber and Faber Limited
The Bindery, 51 Hatton Garden
London EC1N 8HN

Typeset by Brighton Gray
Printed and bound in the UK by CPI Group (Ltd), Croydon CR0 4YY

A CIP record for this book
is available from the British Library

ISBN 978-0-571-38278-1

2 4 6 8 10 9 7 5 3

Acknowledgements

With thanks to Mel, Roxana, Greg, Owen, Calam, Izzy, Kit, the Godwin family and everyone at Hampstead Theatre. And special thanks to Gemma and Lucas for their patience during this first production.

Linck & Mülhahn was first performed at Hampstead Theatre, London, on 27 January 2023. The cast was as follows:

Johan / Man 1 / Juryman 1 / Soldier 2 Daniel Abbott
Anastasius Linck Maggie Bain
Mother Lucy Black
Doctor / Market Trader / Man 2 / Priest / Soldier 3 David Carr
Spinster / Lady / Clerk Marty Cruickshank
Captain / Judge Kammy Darweish
Soldier 1 Qasim Mahmood
Girl / Maid Leigh Quinn
Cornelius / Juryman 2 / Executioner Timothy Speyer
Catharina Mülhahn Helena Wilson

Director Owen Horsley
Designer Simon Wells
Lighting Matt Daw
Sound Max Pappenheim
Movement Natasha Harrison
Fight and Intimacy Rachel Bown-Williams and Ruth Cooper Brown of RC-Annie Ltd
Casting Helena Palmer CDG

For Cal

Characters

Spinster
Anastasius Linck
Catharina Mülhahn

Girl
Mother
Soldier
Captain
Maid
Doctor
Johan
Lady
Cornelius
Judge
Juryman 1
Juryman 2

Troops, Market Trader, Men, Priests, Executioner

LINCK & MÜLHAHN

Note

The world of Acts One to Three is dimly lit, with the
tenebrous magic of a painting by the likes of Joseph Wright
of Derby. It has a slightly worn, homely quality to it, but
there is also a febrile, glowing mystery in its dark corners
and secret encounters. By contrast, the second world (of
Acts Four and Five) should feel bright, clinical and almost
ahistorical, with less room to hide.

*

Doubling is encouraged.

*

My only hard and fast rule for casting is that Anastasius
should be played by a queer actor e.g. not a cis heterosexual
male or female. This is not up for debate.

*

– indicates an interruption.

. . . at the end of a line of dialogue indicates trailing off,
unable to find the words.

A new line indicates a new thought.

A forward slash / indicates where the next line overlaps.

A blank space in place of a printed line indicates a beat of
silence.

Act One

A shiver of cello music [I like to imagine '4.3 Courante' from Bach: The Cello Suites recomposed by Peter Gregson].

The late eighteenth century. In a small, poorly lit room, a Spinster sits at a spinning wheel.

Spinster Tick. Tick. Tick.
Have you ever in your life looked up, and seen that it is not minutes, but years that have passed? There is a great turning in your stomach as you realise – you are old.
And what do you have to show for it?
Wrinkles and regret.

Hark at me, I sound a right old curmudgeon. A true spinster.
I have spent many a long year on regret.
Now I feel the thread of my life running short. I must try, for the first time, and perhaps the last, to speak the truth.
It is what he wanted.

A strange thing, truth. I often think it resembles a web, that catches you no matter what. For if I were to say, 'We cannot know what happened, for there is no such thing as truth,' you would say, 'Ah, but then, how do you know that to be true?' Tricky.
The best I can do is tell you what I remember.

I ought to start with the first time I saw him.

Across a gauzy veil of time, a warm, gorgeous light rises gradually on a dashing soldier in military dress.

He wore the uniform of the Hanoverian troops – which I must say I always admired.

3

I would leave my sewing and go to the window when they rode by, and mother would strike me with her embroidery frame.
Or the poker.
Or whatever she was holding at the time.

By god did he look fine.
White worsted stockings, up to the knee.
Gaiters over the stockings, buttoned up the side.
Shoes of cow's leather, with thick heels and brass buckles.
White shirt of oznabrig. Billowing.
White linen breeches. Snug.
Navy frock coat, with red collar and cuffs.
And a black felt hat, with a puschel – a pompom, on top.

On the other side of the stage a young woman, who bears a striking resemblance to the Spinster, appears.

Sometimes I look back on that first moment I saw him, and it is as if I had been living my life half in shadow. Then suddenly – there was light.

But I am getting ahead of myself. I must first set the scene.

The two figures come to life. The girl takes out a book and a peach. The soldier is handed a flagon of mead.

It begins with two strangers. In the year of our lord 1720. A soldier at a dance, out Gehowen way. And a girl, hiding in her pantry in Halberstadt.
Their lives will meet and intertwine, weaving a story of great passion. There will be suffering and there will be beauty.

But that is all I can tell you. The rest you must imagine for yourselves.

A raucous dance spills across the stage. A woman flashes her bloomers. A man downs his flagon of mead. Everyone is having the time of their lives. The soldier from the Prologue is swept up in it. This is our hero Anastasius, a charming, enigmatic cad. They begin dancing with a Girl.

Split scene: in a pantry, the woman from the Prologue sits reading her book and eating a peach. This is our heroine Catharina, a spirited person who longs for something more.

Meanwhile: in a quiet corner off the dance-hall the soldier embraces the Girl. She has an orgasm.

Girl God's wounds!

Anastasius Quite.

Girl I never knew pleasure like it.

That thing you do with your hand . . .

Anastasius Years of practice.

Girl That I can tell.
Now, what might I do for you?

Anastasius For me?

Girl Surely you wish to have your pleasure too.

Anastasius I took my pleasure in watching yours.

Girl And you a man? I never heard the like.
Give it here.

She reaches for their breeches. They back away.

Anastasius I beg you do not.

Girl 'Tis all the same to me. Saves me the gin and hot water.

Anastasius puts on their hat.

5

Might we meet again?

Anastasius I am afraid not. My regiment marches
tomorrow.

Girl A shame.

Anastasius But I will hold these fleeting moments we have
shared forever in my heart.
And with that, fair maid, adieu.

Girl Not so fast. That'll be forty thalers.

Anastasius Beg pardon?

Girl Forty.
Thalers.
The coins you use to pay for things.

Anastasius But . . .

Girl You did not think I was –

Anastasius A lady's maid? A parlourmaid? Here for the
dance –

Girl I am a tail.

Anastasius But. You look so clean –

Girl I wash.
Monthly.

Anastasius Your face is fair.

Girl Paint and powder. You can barely make out the pox
scars, see?

Anastasius You ought to make yourself known.

Girl Ah, but people see what they wish to see.

Pay up, sir. I have three toothless babes and no husband
to speak on.

Anastasius But –

Girl Do not try my patience.
I will gladly go out there and shout rape.
Or papist, that they may move quicker.

Anastasius Alright, alright.

They hand her some money.

Girl My thanks.

Forgive me if I misled you. A girl must make a living somehow.

Anastasius I quite understand.

Girl If you weren't such a good fuck, I would swear you were born yesterday.

She marches out, leaving Anastasius standing.
In Catharina's world, a voice shouts from offstage.

Mother (*off*) Catharina?

Catharina Yes, Mother –

Mother (*off*) Catharina!

Catharina I'M COMING!

She stomps off.

2

An army barracks. Anastasius spars with a fellow Soldier,
an earnest young man and a true friend. The Soldier is
trying not to laugh as he fights.

Anastasius Rosenstengel.

The soldier laughs harder.

Enough, Rosenstengel. This is no cause for mirth.

Anastasius jabs at the Soldier, who falls on his back and
lies there, laughing uncontrollably.

Anastasius I was made to look a fool.

Soldier That is what is so funny.

Anastasius I take great pride in my ability to woo a woman through wit, not through my purse.

Soldier It is the state of her purse you should be worried about.

Anastasius Such disrespect!

Anastasius keeps practising their fencing moves, while the Soldier lounges on the ground.

Just because you could not get a woman a-bed for a thousand thalers.

Soldier I do not wish to.
I would rather wait.

Anastasius (*snorts*) You will disappoint her.

Soldier Who?

Anastasius Your wife.
She will be expecting a stallion and be met with a – a lapdog.

Soldier As long as I am in her lap I warrant she won't complain.

Anastasius You will be clumsy with her. A novice.

Soldier We will learn together.

Anastasius Loving takes practice. It is an art. As with fighting, and with dice –

Soldier No. Love is no art. It is inborn. Like . . . like a taper inside each of us, waiting to be lit. And our beloved is the flame. Once the two meet, they illuminate the darkness. Like . . . lightning over a field. Moonlight bathing a lake.

Anastasius Hogwash.

Soldier Anastasius. You are so insensible.

Anastasius I am unsentimental. There is a difference.
En garde.

Anastasius proffers their weapon. The Soldier ignores it.

Soldier Do you truly not believe in love?

Anastasius I do not believe . . . in the signs they call love.
The blushing cheek. The amorous glance. The heart that
beats a-pace. These are mere seeming.
A person's soul is their true self. And that cannot be seen.
You can never truly know another. Therefore love is but
a sham.

Soldier What of – maternal love?

Anastasius Ah, you forget, Rosenstengel. My mother was a
poor unfortunate, who left me on a church step for nuns
to find.

Soldier Because she loved you!

Anastasius Because she could not.
'Mother'. 'Love'. These are but words. In the end we
have no one but ourselves.

Soldier You know, you remind me of my uncle.

Anastasius Is he terribly handsome?

Soldier He too is all ideas. He reads Mr Locke, Descartes,
Leibniz –

Anastasius Fine thinkers.

Soldier He pretends he is all head. But I can tell beneath he
has a heart.
See, here he writes and calls me 'son'. Asks when I may
visit him.

He gets out a letter and shows Anastasius, who takes it.

9

Anastasius Let me see that.

Cornelius Rosenstengel.

Soldier He is a clothmaker. Out in Gültenberg, near Prague.

Anastasius I should like to be a clothmaker, were I not a
soldier. To fashion beauty out of nothing.
And I am good with my hands.

Soldier You are a rake.

Anastasius Do you know what you are?

Soldier What?

Anastasius A sissy. Your uncle too.

Soldier A sissy?

Anastasius A sissy, a molly and a sap.

Soldier En garde.

Anastasius Oh, so now you want to fight? With the best
swordsman in the barracks?

Soldier En garde.

Anastasius Very well.
Prêt?
Allez.

*They spar. Anastasius is by far the better fighter; they
barely have to try.*
*The Soldier puts up a decent – if effortful – resistance,
then ends up on his back again.*

Soldier I surrender! I surrender.

Anastasius See? Sissy.

Soldier Help me get up.

Anastasius Get yourself up. You must be good enough at it
by now.

The Soldier laughs.

Soldier One day I wager you will fall in love. Then you will change your tune.

Anastasius Wager what?

The Soldier thinks. Then:

Soldier My silk cravat.

Anastasius The yellow moire? That is a fine cravat.

Soldier I know it. It is yours upon your wedding day.

He holds out his hand. Anastasius shakes it and pulls him to his feet.

Anastasius Knave. I shall never marry. Not unless I meet a girl who can see beyond the carapace into my soul. And no such wench exists.

3

Catharina is in her parlour staring out of the window. Mother, a woman preoccupied by appearances, sits embroidering nearby.

Catharina I wish I were dead.

Mother Tush. That is blasphemy.

Catharina What is the point of being alive? All I do is sit. Take a turn about the garden. Sit some more. I may as well be dead.

Mother Play a tune on the harpsichord. Your dear departed father always loved it when you played.

Catharina I'd rather stick pins in my eyes.

Mother Try some embroidery.

Catharina Then I would have pins to hand and that would seal my fate.

A grandfather clock ticks.

Tick. Tick. Tick. That clock.
How is it only a quarter off one?

Mother Nearly luncheon.

Catharina Then tea. Then dinner. Then breakfast once again. The days of my life drift by like bubbles. Before I know it I will be five-and-twenty and then I will die and I will have done nothing except watch that damn clock –

Mother Such drama. If it was not immodest I should suggest you take to the stage.

Catharina I would love to be an actress.
Or a woman of letters.

Mother Tush. Reading makes you cross-eyed.

Catharina Says who?

Mother And it debauches the mind.

Catharina I long for some debauchery.

Mother You know what leads to excitement . . .

Catharina Don't. Don't say it –

Mother The greatest excitement in a woman's / life is marriage.

Catharina If you say marriage I will lift up my skirts and crap right here upon the hearth.

Mother Catharina. Don't be grotesque.

Catharina Rather be grotesque than boring.

Mother Then you shall die alone.

Catharina Rather die alone than live a life of tedium shackled to some brainless booby.

Mother You are insufferable.

Catharina And you are getting lines by your eyes.

Mother Tush!

Catharina It is true. I can see them by the light of this
window.

Mother tries to contain herself but . . .
  She cannot.

Mother You . . . devil.

She rushes out of the room to check her lines.

Catharina smiles.
  She takes her chair to the window, kneels on it and
looks out. Perhaps we can hear the sound of the street.
There are soldiers marching by.

Mother rushes back in.

Catharina! Catha—
Whatever are you doing?

Catharina Just – looking. There is a regiment passing by.

Mother It does not do to look. You may be seen.
  Johan Pieterson is here. I saw his hackney carriage
  coming down the lane. Get down from there.

Catharina One moment –

Mother hits Catharina with her embroidery frame.

Mother Now.
  Go and do something with your hair.

Catharina Like what?

Mother Powder it.
  And hide the patches on your dress. You need a new one.

Catharina I like this one. It is comfortable.

Mother Go.

Catharina I will go upstairs. And I will submit to a new dress. If you let me read for an hour each day this week.

Mother Catharina –

Catharina Fine. I shall stay here. With my bad hair. And I think I feel a fart coming . . .

Mother Fie. You – harpy –

Catharina Takes one to know one.

Mother You may read your book. But only by the light of the window, to save your eyes.
And the design of your dress shall be of my choosing.

Catharina My thanks, Mama.

She goes.

Mother Do not be long! You mustn't keep Mr Pieterson waiting!

She sits to receive her visitors, striking an 'attractive' pose. Then she remembers the lines. Quickly smooths them out with her fingers. Satisfied.

Lines. Poppycock.

4

Anastasius and the Soldier stand to attention in a line of Troops under inspection by a Captain.

Captain Gentlemen of the Regiment of Hanoverian Musketeers. It has come to my attention that some of you have been fraternising with peasants. Soldiers in uniform were seen at a local dance indulging in wine, women and song.

Anastasius smirks at the Soldier while the Captain's back is turned.

This is unacceptable, not least because plague is on the rise. Thus, we will be enforcing full medical examinations of every soldier within the week.

Anastasius But sir –

Captain Corporal Linck, is there a problem?

Anastasius None of us have symptoms, sir.

Captain Are you a doctor, Linck?

Anastasius No sir.

Captain Well Dr Francken fucking is.
Stand to attention.

Anastasius does so. The Captain shouts in their face.

HOW MANY MEN, WOMEN AND CHILDREN DID OUR FINE COUNTRY LOSE IN THE PLAGUE OF 1710?

Anastasius . . .

Captain HOW MANY, BOY?

Anastasius I do not know, sir.

Captain ONE HUNDRED AND EIGHTY-EIGHT THOUSAND. THAT IS A THIRD OF OUR POPULACE, BOY.

Anastasius Sir.

Captain ARE YOU A FUCKING SAINT?

Anastasius No, sir.

Captain ARE YOU A FUCKING CORPSE?

Anastasius No, sir.

Captain ARE YOU A FUCKING LOAF OF BREAD?

Anastasius No, sir.

Captain THEN YOU CAN CATCH THE FUCKING PLAGUE, BOY. AND YOU WILL BE EXAMINED BY DR FRANCKEN WITH THE REST OF US.

Anastasius Yes, sir.

The Captain comes close to Anastasius.

Captain I am going to ask Dr Francken to pay special attention in your examination. I wish to know how many hairs there are on those pearly smooth balls of yours. Ganymede.

Anastasius keeps their cool.

ATTENTION.

The Troops snap to attention.

MARCH.

They goose-step.

5

Catharina stands in her underclothes with a wide pannier on top. A Maid is fastening the pannier. Mother fusses.

Catharina I look like a milkmaid.

Mother They call it a pannier. It is terribly au courant in France.

Catharina So's bigamy.

The Maid snorts.

Mother Gerthe.

Maid Ma'am.

Catharina No doubt it was invented by some monstrous ass who wished to prevent women from escaping through doorways.

Mother Tush.

Catharina It resembles nothing so much as a chicken basket, of the kind one sees in the market. Here am I, trussed up like a chicken.

Catharina clucks like a chicken.
The Maid snorts again.

Mother Gerthe.

Maid Ma'am.

Mother Fetch me the tape.

The Maid goes.

I cannot quite believe I am having to fashion you a dress myself, but times being what they are, and your dear father –

Catharina Yes, how ill-mannered of him to die. Before I was even ten.

Mother Do not speak ill of him.

Catharina I only mean he left me without a dowry. You could have had me married off by twelve. Now look at me, twenty-two and crabbed with age.

Mother If we lower the bodice like so –

Catharina I shan't be able to bend over.

Mother Why on earth would you want to do that?

The Maid returns with a measuring tape and hands it to Mother, who measures.

Split scene: in another part of the stage, Anastasius appears at the barracks, being examined (fully clothed) by a Doctor.

Doctor Say 'ah'.

Anastasius Ah.

Doctor Very good.

During the following the Doctor peers beneath Anastasius's eyelids, then hits them on the knees to check their reflexes.

Mother We must tighten your stays.

Catharina Why?

Mother They hang quite loose.

Catharina That is how I like them.

Mother Come, Catharina, we cannot measure your true size, the dress will be enormous.

Catharina bites her tongue. Mother and the Maid set about tightening her corset. It is rough, physical work. Catharina hates every second.

Doctor Your reflexes are good. Your humours appear balanced.
Now, undress.

Anastasius No.

Doctor No?

Anastasius I do not wish to.

Doctor It is not a question of wishing, Corporal Linck –

Anastasius I refuse to undress.

Doctor Then I shall make you.

Anastasius Really? How?

Catharina gasps.

Mother Hold still.

Doctor Well . . . I will . . . call for the Captain.

Anastasius Will you?

Doctor Yes.

Anastasius Very well.
Before you do, I should warn you, the minute you call for him I will kill you.

Anastasius takes out their rapier calmly.

I will cut a seam down your body, from your chin to the base of your stomach.

Doctor I say . . .

The Doctor tries to escape.
Quick as a flash, Anastasius has him in a hold, the rapier to his throat.

Anastasius (*tuts*) That was very unwise, Doctor.
Now, I am going to leave this room. Then I am going to leave the barracks. Then I am going to leave this town. You will not report me for deserting. If you betray my wishes, I will find you, cut off your measly member, and choke you with it. Is that clear?

The Doctor squeaks.

I said, is that clear?

Doctor Yes.

Anastasius Marvellous.

Anastasius edges towards the door, without taking their eyes off the Doctor.

Catharina I cannot breathe.

Mother Tush, Catharina –

Catharina It is not a jest –

Mother Such hysterics. No one will marry a girl given to such flights of fancy.

Catharina I must get some air.

Mother But you are only half dressed –

Catharina Let me go.

Catharina breaks away from Mother and runs outside. Meanwhile, Anastasius escapes from the barracks.

A shiver of cello music. For a moment everything dissolves except the two of them: Catharina on her doorstep, gulping in air. Anastasius running as fast as they can.

The Spinster enters and watches them. This is the moment she described in the Prologue. The first moment she saw them.

Anastasius stops for a moment to catch their breath. They lock eyes with Catharina. A moment of pure electricity.

Then Mother appears and grabs Catharina.

Mother Catharina, come back inside this instant. The neighbours might see you.

She pulls her back in.

The Spinster watches as Anastasius lets their breathing settle for a moment.

They stare out ahead of them, preparing for a new chapter. Then march on.

6

Mother stands in the parlour with Johan, who has a permanent foolish grin.

Johan Is that a pianoforte?

Mother A harpsichord, I believe.

Johan Rather.

Mother Catharina's musical talents are quite refined. She takes after her father in that regard. I must ask her to play for you.
She is also skilled at embroidery.
And her singing is exquisite.

Johan Rather.

Catharina enters.

Mother Catharina Margaretha. Johan has honoured us with a call. Won't you play him a ditty on the harpsichord?

Catharina I'm afraid I must absent myself. To purchase the silk for my new dress?

Mother But child, you can / certainly –

Catharina It would be a terrible shame if I did not have it for the assembly next month. I am sure Johan would not wish to accompany me in a tatty, patched old gown.

Johan (*ecstatic*) Accompany you . . .

Catharina (*'innocent'*) Forgive my presumption. I was hoping you might?

Johan I . . . I mean I . . . I would be honoured / to –

Catharina Good.
Mother?

A brief, acid stand-off between Catharina and Mother.

Mother Very well. But Gerthe must accompany you.

Catharina Naturally. I am not a common slut.

Mother and Johan gasp.

Catharina À bientôt!

Catharina leaves.
An awkward beat.

Mother Well. Since you came all this way you must stay for tea.

Johan And cake perhaps?

They disappear.

We find Catharina on the street with the Maid.

Catharina Now, goody Gerthe. I happen to know you have a fondness for ale –

Maid (*panicked*) Ma'am, please, I take only a sip from the pantry here and / there –

Catharina Do not panic. We all have our pleasures.
Here's ten thalers. Go to the alehouse and meet me back here at three thirty.

The Maid takes the money and goes.

Catharina sighs happily.

Finally.

She spreads out her arms. Breathes in the air.

A Market Trader walks past with a chicken in a basket.
It clucks at Catharina. She clucks back.

She does a little dance, twirling around.

Act Two

A clothmaker's. The bell rings as Catharina twirls into the shop. Anastasius stands behind the counter, now dressed as a merchant instead of a soldier.

Catharina It is you.

Anastasius Me?

Catharina The Hanoverian.
  You ran past my house. You looked quite distressed –

Anastasius I am afraid you must have me mistaken for someone else.

Catharina I do not.
  I'd know that uniform anywhere.

Anastasius Is that so?

Catharina Navy frock coat.
  White shirt of oznabrig. Billowing.
  White linen breeches. Snug.

Anastasius You spend a lot of time looking at soldiers?

Catharina As much as I reasonably can.

Anastasius (*enjoying her*) I wish I could satisfy you. I am but a lowly clothmaker.

Catharina I know the clothmaker here. His name is Bergholtz.

Anastasius My new employer.

Catharina Bergholtz never hired a man before.

Anastasius He never met me.

They eye each other, intrigued.

Catharina You are a soldier.

Anastasius I am not.

Catharina Then you have transmuted overnight.

Anastasius Perhaps.

Catharina Only papists believe in transmutation.

Anastasius Perhaps I am a papist.

Catharina Scandal.

Anastasius Or perhaps you merely saw me in your sleep.

Catharina My sleep?
You mean my dreams?

Anastasius I am too modest for such a claim.

Catharina A modest man? What use is that, pray tell?

Anastasius You prefer a coxcomb?

Catharina I prefer a cock. Who crows. That the hens know where to find him.

Anastasius Then he should be hen-pecked.

Catharina Better to be pecked than poxed, by resorting to whores.

Anastasius I assure you, madam, I am pox-free. In fine fettle.

Catharina Fine fighting fettle? Then you are a soldier?

Anastasius A soldier slain by love of you, perhaps.

Catharina Touché. Is that not what soldiers say?

Anastasius If 'touché' is French for touch, then sign me up.

Catharina smiles.

Catharina Well this is fun.

The shop's bell rings. A snooty Lady, with an elaborate fan lorgnette that she likes to peer through, enters.
    She looks Catharina up and down haughtily.
Catharina curtsies.

Lady Hmm.

Anastasius hurries to serve the Lady, kissing her hand.

Anastasius Mrs Von Crayen. More radiant each day than the last.

Lady You only met me yesterday.

Anastasius Then imagine my excitement at what may greet me tomorrow.

Lady I am here to collect –

Anastasius Ten yards of linen with pink sprigs and our finest muslin fichu. Who could forget such exquisite taste?

They bow.
    Catharina pretends to browse, loving eavesdropping.

Lady What did you say your name was?

Anastasius Anastasius Lagrantinus Rosenstengel. Of Gültenberg, near Prague.

Lady Quite a mouthful.

Anastasius I'm afraid so.

Lady Perhaps next time you can deliver?

Anastasius And let me assure you, madam, I always do.

They hand the Lady her parcel and she leaves. Anastasius
waves her off charmingly.
  The shop's bell rings.

Catharina So you are a coxcomb. I have always wanted to
see one in the flesh.

Anastasius My clothes prevent that.

Catharina More's the pity.

Sparks fly.

Anastasius To what do I owe the pleasure of your custom?

Catharina I need silk.

Anastasius Naturally. Skin so fine should be met with
finery.

Catharina Bootlicker.

Anastasius I merely say what I see.
We have a very elegant brocade from Lyon. Or a floral
weave by a lady designer from / England –

Catharina I want something . . . irresistible.

Anastasius Ah.

Catharina My mother cares for how things look. I care
only for how they feel.
(*Seductively.*) It should be like gossamer. That slides
through my fingers like the petals of a flower just opened.
Aching to be plucked.

A beat when it almost seems as if they might kiss.
  Then Catharina pulls back.

Do you have such a thing?

Anastasius clears their throat.

Anastasius Yes – uh . . . but not in stock. A damask. I can
order it for you to collect next week?

Catharina I shall.
  Good day, Mr Rosenstengel.

Anastasius What should I call you?
  Aphrodite perhaps?

Catharina Then you are Adonis.

Anastasius A mere mortal. And you a goddess, for whom
  I would give my life.

Catharina Steady on.
  Catharina Margaretha Mülhahn.

Anastasius Catharina Margaretha?

Catharina Yes. Do you like the name?

Anastasius It is . . . familiar.

A beat as Anastasius thinks about something and
Catharina tries to work out what it is.
    Then they are all charm again.

I hope it will be more so soon.
Miss Mülhahn.

Catharina curtsies, then leaves.

Another shiver of cello music.

Catharina Margaretha . . .

2

Catharina on her way out of the house, humming gleefully.
She bumps into Mother and Johan by the door.

Mother Catharina. Such generosity. Johan has called to
  take you for a ride in his hackney carriage.

Catharina I am afraid I get carriage sick.

Mother You do not.

Catharina It is a – new malady.
Last time I had eaten pigs' feet and they came right back up and exploded / all down my –

Mother Well then – Johan, I beseech you, at least stay for dinner.

Johan If it shall please Miss Mülhahn . . .

Catharina It pleases me greatly.

Mother Good.

Catharina I should hate to think of Mama dining alone.

Mother Alone?

Catharina Since I must absent myself.

Mother But – where are you going?

Catharina I promised Mr Bergholtz I would pick up the silks.

Mother But Gerthe is busy cooking –

Catharina Then I shall excuse her from accompanying me. She does work so very hard after all.

Catharina leaves.

Mother Catharina!

From out of the darkness, breathlessly . . .

Anastasius (*off*) Miss Mülhahn . . .

Johan offers Mother his arm, smiling dumbly.

Johan Shall we?
Something smells delicious. Pigs' feet, perhaps?

Mother tries to smile.

Behind the counter at the clothmaker's, Anastasius and Catharina make out passionately.

Anastasius Oh, Miss Mülhahn . . .

Catharina Call me Catharina.

Anastasius Miss Mülhahn sounds more – piquant.

Catharina That thing you are doing with your hand . . .

Anastasius Should I stop?

Catharina No, no, it is – ah – it is quite transporting.

Anastasius Years of practice.

Catharina Then I must practise too.

She reaches for his trousers.

Anastasius Don't.

They back off.

Catharina What is the matter?

Anastasius I do not wish to – try your virtue.

Catharina Fear not. It has been tried before now.

Anastasius Still. The ecstasy of your kiss is sufficient.

Catharina As you please.
But don't let's stop.

They go back to kissing.

The bell rings as the Lady from before enters the shop.
Anastasius and Catharina hide.
The Lady waits.
Clears her throat.

Lady Mr Rosenstengel? I have come to be measured for my new dress.

She preens.
　Catharina lets out a snort of laughter. Anastasius
hushes her.
　The Lady's ears prick up.

Mr Rosenstengel . . .?

Catharina (*giggling*) I am afraid he is . . . indisposed at
present.

Anastasius (*sotto voce*) Catharina!

The Lady takes this in.

Lady Hm.

Then turns on her heel and leaves.
　Catharina dissolves into laughter.

Catharina 'I am here to be measured for my dress.' She is
quite enamoured of you.
You are used to that, I suppose?

Anastasius I have an open heart.

Catharina An open heart that opens legs.

Anastasius You could not conceal yourself if your life
depended on it.

Catharina Why would I wish to conceal myself?
It is as Descartes says. Shame comes from caring too
much for the opinion of others.

Anastasius You have read Descartes?

Catharina I have dabbled.

Anastasius I prefer Locke.

Catharina That old canker.

Anastasius He is a modern man. An empiricist. He holds
that knowledge comes from experience. It is not innate.

Catharina And yet he died a virgin. Some experience.

Anastasius You are quite unlike other maids. You are so . . . bold.

Catharina Urgh, don't use that word.

Anastasius 'Bold'?

Catharina 'Maid.' It is so . . . simpering.
I should rather be a madam than a maid.

Anastasius Is that right?

Catharina pulls Anastasius towards her and they make out some more.

Split scene: the Lady and Mother stand in the parlour. The grandfather clock ticks.

Awkwardness.

Lady Is that a pianoforte?

Mother A harpsichord, I believe.

Lady Oh. It resembles a pianoforte.

Mother Perhaps it is. Or perhaps it merely resembles one. To be perfectly frank my knowledge of music is indifferent at best.

Lady One cannot be indifferent to music. One can only be ignorant.

More awkwardness.

Mother Are you quite sure you will not sit?
Perhaps I can furnish you with some refreshment.
We have some very fine / peaches –

Lady This is not a social call.
I come with a grave warning.

Mother Oh?

Lady I do not wish to meddle in another family's affairs. In matters which threaten to become . . . indelicate, I strive to have no part –

Mother Indelicate?

Lady But your daughter ought to be careful.

Mother Catharina? What the devil has she / done now?

Lady If you could refrain from blasphemy in my presence.

Mother Forgive me.

Lady I shall not say more. But beware of the clothmaker.

Mother Mr Bergholtz?

Lady Lord, no, not that gout-ridden old toad. I mean his apprentice.

Mother I was not acquainted with the fact he had an apprentice.

Lady Perhaps you were not acquainted for a reason.

He is a silver-tongued deceiver. Luring women in with fine words and then cruelly casting them aside . . . Naturally I do not speak from personal experience. Only hearsay.

Mother I see.

Lady She ought to leave him be. If this were known about town, it could have dire consequences. A daughter without a dowry is a burden. A daughter without her chastity is as good as dead.

Catharina has an orgasm.

I bid you good day.

The Lady opens her fan lorgnette grandly. They disappear.

Catharina In the name of all that is holy.

Anastasius Better say an extra Hail Mary tonight.

Catharina Knew you were a papist.
Once a week is simply not enough.

Anastasius chuckles.

Joy is like a bucket with a hole. One must keep filling it over and over.

Anastasius Sounds a plaguey bucket.

Catharina On the contrary. The hole is its greatest pleasure.

Anastasius Sauce-box.

Catharina Cad.

Anastasius Jade.

Catharina Rogue.

Anastasius Pin-box.

Catharina Addle-pate.

Anastasius Baggage.

Catharina I cannot imagine what mother will make of you when she meets you.

Anastasius Why ever would she do that?

Catharina It is inevitable.

Anastasius Is it?

Catharina She will meet you when we are married.

Anastasius Catharina . . .
Marriage was never mentioned.

Catharina I simply presumed –

Anastasius Do not presume when it comes to me.

Catharina But I am utterly enchanted by you.

Anastasius And I by you –

Catharina All these years I have avoided marriage. I would rather be a spinster than a fool's chattel. But with you . . .

Anastasius You have barely made my acquaintance.

Catharina One does not need to make the acquaintance of someone to whom one is – fitted like a key to a lock.

Anastasius Catharina. That is dreadfully naïve.

Catharina I am not . . . Do not think I . . . I do not mean merely the way you look. I mean . . .
Your gait.
The cadence of your speech.
The way you laugh at the same trifling things as I do.
The way you talk wisely upon subjects about which I wish to be wise, and listen keenly when I wish to be heard.
The way you look at me.
The shape of your smile.
Your smell – bergamot and leather –

Anastasius That is mere seeming.

Catharina What else is there?

Anastasius The truth.

Catharina Does not the way one seems reflect one's truth?

Anastasius It is the garment one wears to hide it.

Catharina What of Locke? Empiricism –

Anastasius The limits of empiricism are the limits of what we can see.

Catharina But true love sees beyond –

Anastasius Love is blindness. Folly. It can never go beyond the surface. To a person's essence.

34

Catharina I see your essence.

Anastasius Foolish girl, you do not.

Catharina Then do you not wish to let me?

Anastasius No.
And I do not wish to see yours, either.
I have always been alone. A discarded soul with only
myself to rely on. If I betray myself now . . . then I will
truly have nothing.

I am sorry. Sometimes you must hurt another to be true
to yourself.

Catharina stares at them.

Catharina Wretch.

Anastasius It is for your own good –

Catharina Devil.

Anastasius Perhaps your anger will prove a useful scourge
to this – this impression of love.

Catharina I thought you had more respect –

Anastasius If you measure a man's respect by the time he
spends beneath your skirts, you may need to re-evaluate
your yardstick.

*Catharina picks up a piece of silk and tears it. Then
another.*

Catharina –

She keeps tearing.

Catharina. Stop. This is my livelihood. Mr Bergholtz will
charge me for this.

Catharina Consider it the cost of my company. You have to
pay for whores, don't you?

4

Split scene: left alone in the cloth shop, Anastasius sighs and begins to tidy up.

Meanwhile: Catharina hides in the pantry, hunched on the floor, letting her feelings go.

After a moment, a candle is lit.

Catharina Mother!

Mother is lurking in the corner of the pantry.

What are you lurking in here for?

Mother I do not lurk. It is inelegant. I . . . linger.

So this is where you come to hide. The pantry.

Catharina The house has but five rooms. It is hardly a great mystery.

Mother I found a good deal of peach stones in that corner.

Catharina Oh? Gerthe must be stealing again.
She is always at the ale.

Mother Those peaches are for decoration only. Mind you keep your hands to yourself.

What vexes you?

Catharina Nothing.

Mother Catharina. You never were good at concealing things.

Catharina I wish I was.

Mother And I too.

Is there something you wish to tell me?

Catharina Do you think I am ill-formed?

Mother Ill-formed? How?

Catharina Ugly.
Undesirable.

Mother Well . . .

Mother thinks. For slightly too long.

Well . . .

You are not a classical beauty.
You are somewhat tawnier of complexion than the
fashion dictates.
Your hair is thick.
Your forehead short.
Your eyes do not sparkle so much as they pierce.
But your – deportment is lovely.

Catharina So I am ugly?

Mother Relieve yourself of such childish notions. What
matters is not what you are, but how you appear. Can
you imagine how foolish the great ladies of the Prussian
court should look if we saw them in their shifts and
stays, without paint or pomp?

Catharina But what of a person's essence?

Mother Essence?

Catharina Their true self.

Mother You have been reading again. I told you those
books would do you no good.

Catharina How did you know you were in love with
Father?

Mother I was married to him.

Catharina You married first, then loved after?

Mother Naturally.

I was the middle of three sisters, as you know. Maria was elegant and wry. Ernesta was beautiful, with terribly soft hands and a lovely, foolish laugh. I was quite plain. Dull. So when your father came calling I set my sights on him. I thought, if I am nothing else, I will be married.

Catharina What did it feel like to you? Love?

Mother It felt like . . .

Safety.
Duty.
Compromise.

Catharina Did you never long for something more?

Mother Your father had ten acres when I met him.

Catharina I mean more . . . feeling.

Mother He was a fine man. A fine husband.
He was . . . tall.
He knew how to shoe a horse.
You cannot dine on feelings. You cannot keep warm with fine words. A man who makes you no promises is a leech. He will suck you dry and leave you bloodless.

The silhouette of the Spinster appears, watching Catharina and Mother.

Catharina But what if you feel drawn to him in a way you never felt drawn before?

Mother Fight it. We women are born with nothing, Catharina. Not the clothes on our backs. Not the hairs on our heads. We must take what we can and cling to it, tooth and nail. Choose a life you can hold in your hands, not an 'essence' you cannot touch.

Catharina Perhaps you are right.

Mother I always am. It is my cross to bear.

Let us go and finish your dress for the assembly.
We must hope Johan will still accompany you after your
disdainful behaviour.

Catharina Johan. Urgh.

Mother His farm is fifteen acres.
And he is a good man. And fond of you.

Catharina He is a dunderhead.

Mother I'm glad to hear your spirits are lifting.
This fichu is filthy. We shall need another.

Catharina I could go –

Mother I will send Gerthe to Mr Bergholtz tomorrow. She
will fetch it.
You will not be going there again. Do you understand?

Catharina Yes, Mama.

Mother Good.
Now, go to the harpsichord. I wish to hear something
gay.

The Spinster gazes at Catharina, as . . .

5

*Music plays. At the assembly, couples dance, drab, tight-
lipped and tedious. It is anything but gay. Catharina dances
with Johan.*

Johan Miss Mülhahn, may I take this opportunity to
remark upon your fine deportment?

Catharina You may.

Johan It is . . . quite fine.

Catharina Is that it?

They spin away from one another.

Has anyone ever told you that you have the personality of an overripe fig?

Johan Beg pardon?

And back in.

Catharina (*faux sweet*) I said I do hope they play a jig. I find them quite transporting.

Johan Ah.

They dance in silence for a while.

Anastasius enters the assembly in disguise, wearing a wig and beard. Catharina doesn't see them.

Finally, the dance ends.

Catharina Oh thank god for that.

Johan Pardon?

Catharina I said I must find my cap.

Johan Oh, but allow me to –

Anastasius intercepts. Catharina recognises them, but pretends not to.

Anastasius Miss Mülhahn, I believe?

Catharina Do I know you?

Anastasius By the end of this jig, I hope to persuade you that you ought to.

They offer her their hand.
Johan fumbles good-naturedly.

Johan Well then. I . . . I shall go and hunt down that lost cap.

He bows.
    A jig begins. This is more like it – upbeat, playful.
    They dance.

Anastasius Who is the lapdog?

Catharina My faithful hound, Johan Pieterson. A
merchant's son.

Anastasius He looks like he's been hit up the face with
a bedpan.

Catharina Not all of us are blessed with chins.

Anastasius God would have been kinder if he'd made him
a cradle death.

Catharina snorts, in spite of herself.
    As they dance, their rhythms perfectly matched, the
rest of the world seems to gradually melt away.

May I say, you look divine.

Catharina (*of their disguise*) You look like a pirate.

Anastasius Come for a parley.

Catharina I am all ears.

Anastasius You are all perfection.

Catharina Yawn.

Anastasius Alright. I shall get to the point. I heartily beg
your forgiveness for my thoughtless – nay, wicked words
last week.

Catharina Consider yourself forgiven.
And dismissed.

She twirls away, but they pull her back.

I will not be devoured and discarded, like some succulent
morsel.

Anastasius But you taste so delicious.

Come, Catty –

Catharina Who is Catty?

Anastasius I rather think it suits you. Stroke you and you purr. Scratch you and you hiss.

Catharina Do not banter me. I am not in the spirits for it.

She stops dancing.

Why did you come here?
You have made your indifference to me quite clear.

Anastasius I am not indifferent. Quite the opposite.

Catharina Then you must wish to torment me.

Anastasius I wish to apologise. That we may part on good terms.

Catharina Why must we part?

Anastasius It is for the best.

Catharina Not for me.
I have but three options. Marriage. Poverty. Or filling my apron with stones and walking into the river.
The last is beginning to seem by far the most appealing.

Anastasius Do not say such things.

Catharina Marry me.

Anastasius I cannot.

Catharina Then let us elope. Live in sin. I would love to shock my mother so.

Anastasius That is no better.

Catharina I do not understand.

Anastasius It is for your sake that I refuse.

Catharina My sake? From what are you protecting me? The clap?

Anastasius I do not have the clap.

Catharina Then what?

Anastasius I . . .
There are things you do not know. Things that would alter your view of me entirely. Things that prevent me from making a claim on such a rare, intelligent woman as you.

Catharina You are not making a 'claim'. I am telling you. I love you.

Anastasius You . . . You love me?

Catharina I have loved you ever since the first time you made me laugh.

Anastasius wrestles.
   Then comes to a decision.

Anastasius Then there is something I must tell you.

I . . . I am different.
I am not a man. Nor a woman. I am – something else. Something more.

That first day we met. When you spoke your name . . . Catharina Margaretha. I fell silent because it was once my name too. It is not now.

Now that I have told you, I must bid you adieu.

Catharina Please don't.

I think a part of me always knew I was . . . searching for something, but the thoughts had no flesh or bones to cling to. Now I have met you, I know what I want.

That is, if you want me too.
I cannot offer much. I have no dowry to speak of.
My forehead is short.
I am often sullen.
And I have a frightful addiction to peaches.
But I can promise to love you. Come what may.

Anastasius Brave girl.

Catharina It is you who makes me brave.

Anastasius Fuck it.

Catharina Fuck it?

Anastasius Let us do it. Let us get married.

Catharina throws her arms around Anastasius.

It will not be like other marriages. You know that, Catty? You choose that?

Catharina Sod other marriages. Let's never be like other people.

Anastasius Never.

They dance an ecstatic, gorgeous routine, like Fred and Ginger but weirder. [I like to imagine 'Modern Love' by David Bowie playing.] Our hearts soar with theirs.

Then:

6

The parlour. Catharina and Anastasius stand before Mother. The clock ticks.

Mother A clothmaker?

Anastasius Yes, ma'am. He lives out in Gültenberg, near Prague.

Mother Hmm.

Anastasius brings out the letter the Soldier showed them in Act One, Scene Two.

Anastasius Only lately I received this letter from him. My father, Cornelius. Wishing that I may visit.

Mother takes the letter gingerly between forefinger and thumb.
As she reads, Catharina pinches Anastasius's bottom. They try to cover their reaction.
Catharina snorts.
Mother looks up sharply.

Mother How many acres has he?

Anastasius None, I am afraid. Only his cloth shop.

Mother Hmm.

Anastasius I have written to tell him of the marriage but I fear he may not be well enough to / attend –

Mother Marriage?

Anastasius Yes. I am here to ask for your daughter's hand.

Mother I am afraid my daughter is spoken for.

Catharina Mother –

Mother Johan, my dear. What of Johan?

Catharina Johan has not proposed.

Mother He still may.

Catharina But Anastasius has.

Mother But who is Anastasius?

Anastasius I am.

Mother Yes, thank you, sir. I am aware of who you are but not from whence you came. You seem to have materialised out of the ether.

Anastasius I come from Gültenberg, near Prague.

Mother So you say.

Anastasius I assure you my father is an upstanding man.

Mother But Catharina –

Catharina You always said the greatest excitement in a woman's life is marriage.

Mother But . . . you never listened. I thought perhaps you would remain here. For good.

I must tell you, sir, she is a wilful girl.

Anastasius I know it.

Mother She can be quite . . . savage.

Anastasius As can I.

Mother Why her?

Anastasius Well . . . look at her.

Mother I am looking.

Anastasius Is she not perfection?

Mother I am afraid I see not what you see.

Anastasius That is the magic of it.
  Leibniz said, 'There is nothing truer than happiness and
  nothing happier and sweeter than truth.' For so long,
  I thought that meant there was but one truth, and one
  could not be happy without it. Now I see it is the other
  way around. One finds one's own truth. Your daughter is
  my happiness. To another she may look ordinary. But to
  me she is . . . a thread of gold running through a tired
  cotton world.

Catharina is spellbound.
  Mother is impatient.

Mother That is all well and good, Mr Rosenstengel, but
  she has no dowry.

Anastasius Frankly, Mrs Mülhahn, I don't give a damn.

7

*Anastasius and Catharina get married. [I imagine 'Chapel
of Love' by The Dixie Cups playing.] It is brief: they join
hands. A Priest twirls them about. Confetti is thrown. They
kiss.*
  Mother cannot hide her tears, and doesn't try.

*Suddenly the scene splits. Anastasius leads Catharina into
their garret.*
  Mother is left alone.

Anastasius Be honest.

Catharina It is . . . homely.

Anastasius Speak the truth.

Catharina I am. It is . . . wholesome.

Anastasius It is a garret.

Catharina Well –

Anastasius With but one room, no privy and rats in the rafters.

Catharina (*jokey*) Anywhere is a palace with you.

Anastasius Toady.

Catharina It is better than living with my mother.

Anastasius That I can believe.

Catharina We did it. We are married.

Catharina curtsies playfully.

Husband.

Anastasius bows.

Anastasius Wife.

They fall into each other's arms.

Blackout.

Act Three

Mother sits alone in the parlour, embroidering. The grandfather clock ticks.

She stops, sighs.

Mother Gerthe?
GERTHE!

The Maid hurries in, wiping her hands on her apron.

Did no one call while I was resting?

Maid No, ma'am.

Mother And no letters have come?

Maid None, ma'am.

Mother Very well.

*The Maid hesitates, waiting for more.
Then turns to go.*

Gerthe. Sit with me a while.

The Maid is uncomprehending.

Maid Sit?

Mother Yes, sit, Gerthe, sit. The thing you do on your backside all day in the scullery when you would have me think you are working.

Maid Oh.

Mother I am lonesome. Keep me company.

Nervously, the Maid goes to sit on the floor.

49

Not on the ground, Gerthe. You are not a cow, albeit you are bovine.
Fetch a stool.

The Maid runs and brings on a stool.
She sits nervously, right on the edge of it.

Sit properly, girl, you are trying my nerves, hovering like that.
And straighten your back. Your deportment is risible.

The Maid tries.

Split scene: in the garret Catharina and Anastasius are post-coital, eating their lunch in their undergarments.

Catharina I love the way the light plays on your hair.

Anastasius I was thinking the same of your eyes. In different lights they change their colour, like when one dyes fabric. From hazel to moss to deepest umber.

Catharina We have become nauseating, haven't we?

Anastasius Quite repulsive.

Catharina Vile. Thank heavens no one else can hear us.

Why do you never undress when we make love?

Anastasius I do.

Catharina Not fully. You always keep on your shirt and drawers.
And you go out to the yard to wash.

Anastasius It wakes me up of a morning.

Catharina I love to be nude.

Anastasius I have noticed.

Catharina It makes me feel – proud somehow. Elemental.

Anastasius I feel proud in my clothes. It is how I feel strong.

Catharina You know you have nothing to fear from me?

Anastasius I know.
I suppose . . . after so many years of hiding, it takes time to feel safe.

Catharina nods.

Catharina When did you know? Who you truly were.

Anastasius thinks.

Anastasius It is a strange thing, 'knowing'.
How does one know anything about oneself?
It seems to come in fragments. Like flotsam rising to the surface of deep water.

For me . . . it began with clothes.
In the convent where I grew up there was a nun named Sister Agnes. When I was perhaps nine or ten years old, she saw my discomfort in skirts and gave me breeches and a shirt to wear.
I still remember the first time I stood before the glass and saw myself. I felt . . . breathless.
Then she persuaded the rest to let me cut my hair. Out of modesty, she told them.

We never spoke the truth aloud, but . . . there is a thing that can pass between two people. Something wordless. A sense of knowing and being known. It is both thrilling and terrifying.

Catharina That is what I felt that day in the cloth shop.

Anastasius It was Agnes who helped me find my name.
Quite by accident.
Or so it seemed.

Catharina Oh?

Anastasius She told me the story of Saint Anastasius. A soldier, martyred for refusing to renounce his faith. His name means 'resurrection'.

Catharina What happened to her? Agnes?

Anastasius I do not know.
When I was fourteen they tried to take the clothes from me and I ran. I have been running ever since.

And you, my wife? When did you know who you were?

Catharina In some ways I feel I am still searching.

My house was full of lies.
My father fell down the stairs. After he died, mother and I played out a charade that he was a fine man. A man of character. But he was a drunk. He was unreliable. Sometimes when he got tired he hit us, like an angry child.
I often wonder what would happen if we let the pretence drop, just for a moment. Would we be happier? Or not?

Anastasius It is life's great aim. To find a way to be honest with oneself, even as the world pretends around you.

Each day, our story is spun, like a tapestry. We cannot control the picture. But we choose whether we look on it and say, 'There, look, a beautiful sunrise.' Or, 'There, look, the fires of hell.'

Catharina looks at them.

Then she jumps on them, kissing them.

What is this?

Catharina I wish I could climb inside your head.
Since I cannot, I will get into your drawers –

Anastasius I must to work. Dinnertime is over –

Catharina Once more before you go.

Anastasius Alright, go on.

Anastasius leaps onto the bed, throwing the sheet over them both.

Mother It is no use. It is not the same, Gerthe. You may go.

Maid Go, ma'am?

Mother Yes, go. Leave. Be gone.

The Maid prepares to scarper.

Gerthe. Do you not have family in Gültenberg?

Maid I do. My sister's husband's brother, ma'am. He works the mines down there.

Mother Do you think he could find someone for me? A man by the name of Cornelius Rosenstengel? A clothmaker. I should like to know more about him.

Maid I could ask, ma'am.
For a thaler or two.

Mother Very canny, Gerthe.
Very well. Two thalers it is.

Catharina lets out a peal of laughter from beneath the sheet.

And do something about that hideous noise.

Maid Noise, ma'am?

Mother The grandfather clock. That endless ticking. It is driving me to distraction.

The Maid bows her head and then hurries off.

Split scene: in the parlour, Mother sighs and takes up her embroidery.

In the garret, Catharina emerges from the bed, reading a book.

Catharina Women 'are for the most part wise enough to love their chains, and to discern how very becomingly they fit . . .'

She flicks to another page.

They are 'from their very infancy debarr'd those advantages, with the want of which they are afterwards reproached, and nursed up in those vices which will hereafter be upbraided to them.'

Anastasius Mrs Astell.

Catharina I found it among your things. I have already devoured the Leibniz and the Locke.
But this . . .

Anastasius You like it?

Catharina Admittedly she does not go far enough. She says women must 'practise passive obedience' –

Anastasius You are no woman then.

Catharina But some of her ideas are quite thrilling.

Anastasius Quite.

Catharina She implies that the seeming of 'woman' is merely what we are told a woman should be.
My mother is forever telling me I am unladylike.
My lack of love for pretty things. The way I prefer to lead in dancing. My outspokenness.
And I have no wish to become a mother. I never felt that keening in my womb that other women speak of.

Anastasius I would not wish this world upon a child. It is too full of careless cruelty.

Catharina Then Mrs Astell is right. I need not love my chains. I can break them.

I only wish she had gone further.

Anastasius You ought to write a response.

Catharina Me?
Write?

Anastasius Respond to Mrs Astell. Tell her where she has erred.

Catharina I could not.

Could I?

Anastasius You can read and write, can you not?

Catharina Of course, but –

Anastasius You have wit and flare enough when you speak, why not on the page?

Catharina But . . .
Who would read it?

Anastasius People.
They read Mrs Astell.

Catharina And mock her. Revile her.

Anastasius Let them mock.
If writing is your essence, you must be true to it.

Catharina But . . . when? I must cook and clean –

Anastasius We can divide the duties. I am much the better at cleaning the floors and windows. You are a dab hand at laundry.

Catharina I do like to scrub out my rage.

Anastasius You can go to market and I can cook.
My cooking is far superior to yours.

Catharina Hark at him.

Anastasius You damn near poisoned us with that veal
scallop.

Catharina Ah yes, the scallop. Not my best work.

Anastasius We can share the labour.

Perhaps one day your writing will make money. Then we
could leave this sordid garret and buy a farm. Raise
ducks and geese.

Catharina A utopia.

Anastasius Composed of you and I.

She turns her back to them.

Catharina Unfasten my stays.

Anastasius Again? Catty, I am exhausted –

Catharina No, no, not for that. I wish to remove them.

Anastasius Alright.

Anastasius undoes her stays.

Catharina I shall not wear them any longer.
Nor shall I labour over my toilette. I shall let my hair
hang loose. And I shall never, ever embroider. I shall be
free. In mind and body.

Anastasius Yes you shall.

Catharina I shall be a woman of letters.
What is a life if lived according to false rules?

Anastasius A facsimile.

Catharina A sham.
  What about you?

Anastasius Me?

Catharina What will you let go of? What foolish trappings
  of society?

Anastasius Nothing.

Catharina Nothing?

Anastasius I have all I want. I have a home where I might
  lock the door. I have a wife who is the sky to my earth.
  I have a job that brings me joy. And when I look in the
  glass, I see a person I recognise. That is more than I ever
  thought I would have.

Catharina How lucky we are.

Catharina steps out of her corset.

'Zounds that feels good! My precious little pot belly is
free.

Anastasius To freedom.

Catharina To freedom.

Anastasius Fuck I love you.

They kiss.

*Anastasius leaves and Catharina takes out a quill and
paper and begins to write.*

*Meanwhile: in the parlour the grandfather clock chimes.
The Maid enters.*

Mother Gerthe. You are hovering. Hovering is for gnats,
  not women.

Maid Forgive me, ma'am.
  If I may. I have received a letter.

Mother And what do you desire from me? Congratulations?

Maid It is from my sister's husband's brother, ma'am. In
  Gültenberg, near Prague.

Mother Oh.

Maid He has found the man you search for. Cornelius
  Rosten . . . Rosenstengel.

Mother What does he say of him?

Maid Forgive me, ma'am. I cannot read.

Mother Tush. Give it here.

  Mother snatches the letter.

  Even I struggle to read this. The script is barely legible.
  He says . . . Rosenstengel is a poor man but well respected.
  And . . . he lives alone in the cottage by the chapel.

  Is that all?

Maid You asked but if he knew him.

Mother I must know more. Of his provenance. His family.
  Any marks upon their characters.

Maid I could ask, ma'am.

For a price.

Mother Don't be absurd, Gerthe.

Maid A thaler.
  Or some ale perhaps.

Mother You will receive my good opinion, nothing more.

Maid Then I am afraid I cannot help, ma'am.

Mother How dare you be so wilful.

Very well then. I shall find out myself.

Honestly, Gerthe. Ale? Have some self-respect.

Mother marches out.

The Maid smiles to herself. Then takes great pleasure in knocking Mother's embroidery to the floor and sitting in her seat.

3

Split scene: Anastasius works downstairs in the cloth shop.

Upstairs in the garret: Catharina writes like a demon. Mother stands watching her for a beat.

Mother Catharina?

Catharina, / may I ask –

Catharina But one more moment . . .

She finishes her sentence.

There.

She blows on the ink.

Mother What, pray tell, are you doing?

Catharina What does it look like?

Mother Taking leave of your senses?

Catharina I am writing.

Mother What?

Catharina A pamphlet.

Mother Why?

Catharina So that it may be read.
  It is entitled 'The Tapestry of Sex'.
  Would you like a copy? I could write you an epigraph –

Mother No.
  Thank you.

  Whatever has happened to your hair?

Catharina Do you like it? It is as it was when I awoke.

Mother You look like a madwoman.

Catharina Perhaps I am.

Mother You have not visited lately.
  Your harpsichord is becoming untuned.

Catharina Is it?

Mother You must come and play. I warrant it will not fit in
  your – new quarters.

Catharina I am afraid I have forgotten how.

Mother Forgotten?

  It was your father's you know.

Catharina Perhaps I am not so like him after all.
  Praise god.

Mother Mind your tongue.

Catharina Father never minded his to us.
  He called you lardy. And a slattern.

Mother Only in jest –

Catharina He pulled my hair. And laughed when I sang –

Mother He was . . . playful.

Catharina He lost his land and spent all your coin on
  whisky –

Mother Do not exaggerate.

Catharina He hit you, Mama.

I do not think he was an evil man. I rather think he was
lost. Weighed down by playing 'man of the house'.
But he was not kind. Or honest.
In truth, you have seemed far happier as a widow than
you ever were as a wife.

Perhaps you do not wish to recall. Do not wish to believe
that the man you thought would be your saviour was
really your destruction. But be / honest –

Mother These floors are filthy. You ought to wash them
with vinegar.

Catharina Anastasius does the floors.

Would you like some supper? Anastasius made a fine
spatchcock chicken last night, of which there is some left.
Or a peach perhaps? We have plenty.
We shall have more once I start selling my work.

Mother Why on earth would you do that?

Catharina To make money. The wage Bergholtz pays is
meagre / and –

Mother Surely your husband will not allow that.

Catharina It was his idea.

Mother You ought to be resting, so that you may quicken
with child.

Catharina We do not want children.

Mother You do not . . .
But . . .
What man does not desire a son?

Catharina shrugs.

Catharina. Do you not think there is something . . . not quite right about your husband?

Catharina Not quite right?

Mother Unnatural. This tendency to cook and clean –

Catharina On the contrary. I think he has a finer nature than any man I ever met.

Mother We know little of his provenance.
This father of his –

Catharina What use is provenance? We make our mark upon this world with words and deeds.

Mother You know you can always come home, my child.

Catharina I am home, Mama.

If you are lonely, you are always welcome here.

She hands her a book.

Mother What is this?

Catharina Mrs Astell. I think you may gain something from it. Do let me know what you think.

Speechless, Mother stares at the book. Catharina goes back to her writing.

Downstairs in the shop, the bell rings. The Soldier enters.

Soldier Well, well. My eyes did not deceive me.

Anastasius looks up and is frozen to the spot.

We were marching by and stopped for water. I glanced into a shop and who should I spy but Corporal Linck, / you old devil.

He moves to embrace them.

Anastasius Do not . . .
You cannot be here.

Mother leaves the garret.

Soldier Deserting is a serious crime. I could have you
flogged.
No doubt the captain would relish the opportunity.

Anastasius You must go. Now.

Soldier Come, fool. I will not tell them.
I wish to hear your news. What lucky strumpet did you
follow here? For if I know you, she is sure to be / a
strumpet –

Mother enters.

Anastasius Mrs Mülhahn.

Mother Mr Rosenstengel.

Hearing his own name, the Soldier looks confused.

Soldier Yes?

Do I know you?

Mother I was addressing him.

Anastasius panics.
*A glance between them and the Soldier. Mother
registers it.*

Who is this man?

Anastasius A customer.
If you will excuse me, sir, I will show you our range of
chintz in a moment.

Soldier Thank you.

Anastasius (*to Mother*) Did you not wish to stay for
supper?

Mother I did not.

Anastasius Still. I know how Catharina treasures your visits.

Mother You should look to your wife, sir. She is quite distracted.

Anastasius Distracted?

Mother You would do well to take better care of her.

Anastasius I will do my best.

Mother Do not expect to see me this coming week. I will be going away for some days. There is someone I wish to visit.

Anastasius Ah. I hope your travels will take you somewhere pleasant?

Mother Gültenberg. Near Prague.

The breath dies in Anastasius. For once, they cannot speak.

Good day, 'Mr Rosenstengel'.

She leaves. The bell tinkles.

Soldier You stole my name.

Anastasius tries to distract themself by folding fabrics.

Anastasius I merely borrowed it –

Soldier Why did she speak of Gültenberg?
That is where my uncle lives.

I wondered why you took my letter –

Anastasius I had to get out. I could not stay in the regiment.

Soldier Why not?

Anastasius What if I told you I was not who I said I was?

Soldier No one knows who you are. You are swaddled in mystery –

Anastasius And that is how it must stay.

Soldier But it cannot. You know it cannot. One way or another, the truth will out.

Anastasius wrestles with a piece of cloth, channelling their frustration into it.

Anastasius This linen is falling apart. One loose thread and the whole thing unravels.

Soldier Anastasius –

Anastasius Look, Rosenstengel, I will speak no more of your uncle. I promise. But you must leave. Never speak or think of me again.

Soldier You know they hang men for less.

Anastasius Less than what?

Soldier Desertion.

Your wife, does she know who you truly are?

Anastasius She is the only one who ever has.

Soldier But this mother of hers does not.
Do you not fear her wrath when she discovers?

Anastasius My fear of not having Catharina is greater.

The Soldier nods.
    Then he takes out a beautiful yellow cravat and hands it to Anastasius.

Soldier This is yours. I promised it to you on your wedding day. It seems it is belated.

Anastasius Your yellow cravat.

Anastasius is moved.
  The Soldier turns to leave.
  Then:

Soldier You know, I saw you once. Before dawn. I was taking a piss. You had gone out early to wash. Alone, as you always did. I must admit, I got a fright. I thought some poor unfortunate had found her way into the barracks. Then I realised who it was.

Take care, Anastasius.

4

A small, dimly lit parlour in Gültenberg, near Prague. Cornelius Rosenstengel sits mending some fabric. Mother stands before him.

Mother I must apologise for my visiting unaccompanied. I am a widow, you see –

Cornelius It makes no odds to me.

Mother You keep a – fine home.

Cornelius Is it fine?

Mother Well. It is . . . small. But serviceable. And practical, being so close to the chapel.

A little dark, perhaps. May I light a candle?

Cornelius I prefer not to waste coins on candles. I am blind, you see.

Mother I see.
A blind clothmaker.

Cornelius The eye sees only the surface of the cloth. It is the hands that feel if it is coarse or it is fine.

Mother That is true.

Cornelius I have no victuals to offer ye, but there is some mead in that flagon there if you'd / care for –

Mother Thank you, I am replete.
I have come to speak with you about a pressing matter, Mr Rosenstengel.

Cornelius Pressing, is it?

Mother It is. It concerns a man who claims to be your son.

Cornelius My son?

Mother His name is Anastasius Lagrantinus Rosenstengel. He works as a clothmaker in Halberstadt.
He has married my daughter –

Cornelius Your daughter?

Mother I must confess, ever since I met him something about him did not – sit right with me. But I'm afraid my daughter was quite besotted, and since no one else was clamouring for her hand –
But I digress. At first my – suspicions were merely in regards to his provenance. I thought he may be poor or –
Not that I judge poverty –

Cornelius They say it is easier for a camel to pass through the eye of a needle than for –

Mother A rich man to enter heaven, yes, I know.
My point being, I only suspected his origins. But now I find myself suspecting him of some graver subterfuge. I come to you as a last port of call. If you can endorse him as your own then I will accept my daughter's fate. If you cannot . . .

Cornelius Madam.
I hope I will not be damned by damning another.
But I can only speak the truth. I have no son.

I had a wife. She died in childbirth some two score year
ago. The child did not survive.

Mother You . . . You have no son?

Cornelius Whomsoever is married to your daughter. It ain't
no son of mine.

5

*The garret. A copper bath steams with water. Catharina is
in it, washing herself. Anastasius sits on her bed, reading her
writing.*

Anastasius Catharina. This is . . . It is so wise and yet so
full of wit. As if you hold your pen lightly –

Catharina I confess I do not. Look at my hand. It is frozen
into a veritable claw.
I have never worked so hard.
Nor felt such satisfaction.

Anastasius (*mock offended*) Never?

Catharina Except a-bed with you, fool.

Will you do my back?

*Anastasius goes and washes her back for her. It is calm,
intimate, daily.*

Anastasius Lift up your hair.

She does, so they can wash her neck.

There.

She settles back into the water.

Catharina This. This is happiness.

Anastasius Having a servant to wash you?

Catharina No, silly. This. Lying in a bath tub. Listening to the rain. With someone you love with every fibre of your being.
People strive, they write pamphlets and wage wars and inspect cadavers, searching for this thing that is right in front of their faces.

Anastasius You are being repulsive again.

Catharina But I am right.

Catharina gets out of the bath, pulling on a slip.

Shall I leave the water?

Anastasius No. I will wash outside, as always.

Catharina Suit yourself.

Anastasius Or . . .

Perhaps I will not.

Catharina Get in. It is good and warm.

Catharina lies on the bed to read.

Anastasius takes a deep breath, then begins to undress.
They step into the bath and put the last of their clothes aside.
They lean back and take a deep breath.

How is it?

Anastasius Heavenly.

Catharina I told you you would like it once you tried it. All
this flinging cold water over yourself from a bowl at
dawn. It is far too monkish.

Anastasius Will you do my back?

Catharina Of course.

She goes over and picks up the cloth.

Your shirt. You have removed it.

Anastasius Yes.

Catharina To what do I owe this honour?

Anastasius You were right. There was one last trapping of
society I had not let go of. I do not want to look back on
my life and know I held on to any shame.

Catharina nods.
She takes their hand and kisses it.
*Then slowly, lovingly, with the utmost care, she
washes them.*

Catharina Sit forward a little.

She continues.

There are three hard knocks on the door of the garret, so loud they seem almost otherworldly. A sepia light floods the scene, as if it has been trapped in amber.

Mother CATHARINA!

Anastasius and Catharina stop and look at each other.

Then they leap out of the bath and pull on their clothes.

Anastasius Catty –

Catharina What is it? What's the matter?

Anastasius Listen to me. You must tell them you did not know. Any of it. The desertion. My name. My identity –

Another three huge, frightening knocks.

Catharina What do you mean? Who is out there?

Anastasius When they ask you, say you did not know.

Catharina Know?

Anastasius Tell them I concealed myself.
Tell them I deceived you.

Catharina I . . . I cannot –

Anastasius Whatever they say, remember this, here, now. Remember what happiness looks like.

Catharina Anastasius –

The door bursts open and two men enter, followed by Mother.

Mother That is him.

Catharina Mother!
What on earth are you –

Mother Stay back, Catharina. Your husband is a fraud. He has lied about his provenance –

Catharina I told you I do not care / about –

Anastasius Do what you want with me but leave her be.

Mother Do not speak to me of my child. You stole her from me. My most precious possession.

Catharina He did not steal me. I left.

Mother I know what you are. You wretch. You creature. You perverse – thing. I had my suspicions but now I know I was not mistaken. You are . . .

I cannot say it. Show her. Show her what you are.

Anastasius does not move.

Hold him down.

The men wrestle Anastasius and get them into a hold.

Catharina Mother! Let him be.

Mother Show her.
Or I will.

Anastasius stands their ground.

Very well.

The Mother holds her hand out to one of the men, who hands her his rapier.
She slices Anastasius's shirt open. Catharina screams, thinking they have been hurt.

Catharina Stop.

Mother See? Fool! See what he is?

Mother goes close to Anastasius.

You disgust me.

She spits.

Now. Come, Catharina.

Anastasius Catty. Go.

Catharina I . . .

Catharina is torn.

The Spinster appears, watching.

Mother Catharina?

Catharina allows the Mother to lead her away.

The Spinster gazes at Anastasius. For the first time, they meet her gaze.

Spinster I left him in their hands that day. I turned my back and walked away.

That is the truth. May god have mercy on my soul.

Bright lights and loud music.

Anastasius is dragged off, struggling for their life.

Blackout.

Act Four

I

A courtroom. It feels bright and timeless, by contrast to the dim, faintly magical world of before.

In the centre, high up, a lectern and a gavel await the Judge.

Below his seat, to one side, there is a witness box.

Lower down, the defendants sit separately. Anastasius is shackled. Catharina is unbound, her head bowed.

Seated on the other side are two Jurymen. Juryman 1 is louche and canny. Now and then he takes out a pipe and plays with it. Juryman 2 is sincere but ineffectual.

The Spinster stands at the front, playing the role of the Clerk.

Spinster The trial – or so they called it, took place in Halberstadt on the thirteenth day of October, 1721. Anastasius was charged with desertion and sodomy. I was charged with collusion.

I do not think I can tell this part of the story. It is like a thorn in my flesh that the skin has grown over. Do not make me dig it out.

And yet. The thread is spun. I have no choice but to follow it.

Unless –

Juryman 1 All rise.

Everyone in the courtroom stands. The Spinster has no choice but to stand back and watch the proceedings play out.

Juryman 1 The honourable Judge Röper.

A world-weary Judge enters and sits.
   He bangs his gavel three times. It sounds a lot like the knocking from Act Three, Scene Five.

Judge I declare this court is now in session.
   Will the jurymen declare themselves.

Juryman 1 stands briefly. Juryman 2 remains seated.

Jurymen 1 *and* **2** Aye.

Judge We commence with the first witness, Mrs Augusta Mülhahn.

Mother steps into the witness box.

Mrs Mülhahn. It was you who discovered the defendants – in flagrante delicto, was it not?

Mother It was, your honour.

Judge Tell us how it happened.

Mother I merely wished to check on my daughter. She had not been herself lately.
   I entered their garret, quite innocently – alone, and . . .
   He came at me. Threatened me.
   I took hold of his rapier – merely to defend myself.
   I meant only to scare him, but I ripped his shirt, quite by accident, and there I saw . . . I saw . . .

Judge Take your time, Mrs Mülhahn.

Mother My daughter screamed but he did not resist. Some man.
   That, your honour, is why I come before you. To see this . . . this criminal tried in a court of law.

Juryman 1 starts eating a nectarine.

Judge Gentlemen, do either of you have any questions to put to the witness?

Juryman 2 Your honour –

Judge Stand, when you are addressing my court, Beuerlain –

Juryman 2 I apologise, your honour, it is just, I have my gouty leg –

Judge I do not desire to know your medical history, Beuerlain, I simply desire that you and all present follow the rules of the court. Those rules are there to guide us to the truth – they are the very stuff of truth, and said rules dictate that you stand upon addressing the witness. Please stop eating that peach, Arnt, you sound like a boot hitting a field after heavy rain.

Juryman 1 stands briefly.

Juryman 1 Uh, your honour, it is not a peach, it is a nectarine.

The Judge simply cannot be arsed to give this more airtime.

Judge Beuerlain?

Juryman 2 is struggling to heave himself up using a stick. It takes a while.

Finally:

Juryman 2 You claim you ripped the defendant's shirt –

Mother By accident.

Juryman 2 By accident, quite, quite. Beneath said shirt, what did you find?

Mother I found . . . the chest of a woman.

Juryman 2 The chest of a woman?

Mother Yes, sir.

Juryman 2 How could you tell it was that of a woman?

Mother Because . . . because it looked like one.

Juryman 2 I say . . .

Judge Does that mark the end of your questions, Beuerlain?

Juryman 2 It does, your honour.

Judge Then please god be seated.

Juryman 2 seats himself laboriously.

Juryman 1 If I may, your honour?

Juryman 1 struts.

Mrs Mülhahn.

Mother Yes?

Juryman 1 How old are you?

Mother I don't see what that has got to do with –

Judge You must answer, Mrs Mülhahn.

Mother I am . . . (*Hating it.*) four-and-forty.

Juryman 1 Four-and-forty. My. Are you really? I would
never have known.
But hearty for your age?

Mother Well . . .

Juryman 1 You were able to physically wrestle your son-in-
law when he / attacked –

Mother She is not my son –

Juryman 1 Your daughter's husband. So called.

Mother I did not 'wrestle' her. She came at me. I acted in
self-defence –

Juryman 1 But you were able to defend yourself. Alone,
with no assistance?

Mother Yes.

Juryman 1 Then you are hale and hearty.
And you'd harboured suspicions about the defendant for some time?

Mother Yes.

Juryman 1 How long?

Mother Ever since I first saw her.

Juryman 1 What sort of suspicions were they?

Mother Strong ones.

Juryman 1 But of what nature?

Mother I suspected her of . . . of not being what she said she was.

Juryman 1 Of not being male?

Mother Yes.

Juryman 1 You harboured strong suspicions that the defendant was not sexed male, and you a hale and hearty woman, and yet you permitted your daughter – your only daughter –to marry her?

Mother No –

Juryman 1 No, Mrs Mülhahn? Pray, what is it I have said that is untrue?

Mother I did not suspect her sex at first. But her . . . legitimacy.

Juryman 1 Legitimacy?

Mother Her parentage. I suspected that she was of low birth, which she is, and that she had falsified her name, which she had –

Juryman 1 So you suspected her of being poor, not female?

Mother I knew there was something . . . wrong about her.

Juryman 1 I put it to you, Mrs Mülhahn, you stood to benefit from your daughter – who was without a dowry, fatherless – and a wayward girl at that – you stood to benefit from her marriage to a seemingly legitimate merchant – albeit of small means – and on that basis you were willing to overlook your suspicions about Miss Linck's sex.

Mother That is false.

Juryman 1 You wanted rid of your daughter. The burden of a spinster.

Mother I love my daughter. I wanted her to be happy –

Juryman 1 Then why let her do it?

Mother I tried . . . I found her a match. A good match –

Juryman 1 Ah, so it was her doing.
She was wilful. Disobedient.

Mother No –

Juryman 1 You must be aware, madam, that your daughter is on trial too. She stands accused of colluding in the act of sodomy, for which she may be put to death.

Mother My daughter is an innocent.
She never had so much as an – unclean thought in her life.

Juryman 1 Really?

Mother She was always terribly well behaved.
He, he, he must have raped her – forced her / to –

Juryman 1 Raped? How awful.
How do you know?

Mother She would not have – surely she would never have – knowingly –

Juryman 1 Do you believe your daughter is a fool, madam? That she belongs in a madhouse, perhaps?

Mother Certainly not.

Juryman 1 Then how could she not know?

Mother . . .

Juryman 1 Did you not educate her?

Mother I did.
I was always encouraging her to read. Books. Mrs Astell –

Juryman 1 You encouraged her?

Mother Yes . . .

Juryman 1 To read? A book written by a woman who thinks her sex ought to do as they please?

Mother No, I . . . I haven't actually read the book myself –

Juryman 1 Then how odd to bestow it upon your child.

Mother I mean only that she was not raised to be a fool.

Juryman 1 What of your husband?

Mother My – husband?

Juryman 1 God rest his soul.
Was he a – good influence?

Mother Certainly.

Juryman 1 I heard he was partial to drink.

Mother No.

Juryman 1 No?

Mother He never touched it.

Juryman 1 Your neighbour – a Mrs Eriksson – claims she often heard shouting coming from the house.

Mother It must have been the servants.

Juryman 1 So he was an honourable man?

Mother Very. Very honourable. And he was . . .
He never . . .
He always . . .

Juryman 1 Well then it must have been your fault.
It generally is the mother's, I'm afraid.
You either knowingly raised an idiot or a sodomite.
Which is it?

Mother I . . .

Juryman 1 checks his nails casually.

Juryman 1 Think carefully before you answer.
We could have you up on charges of collusion too.

Mother Me?

Juryman 1 You, Mrs Mülhahn.

Mother I – I did what I could.
I did not know they would arrest her too –

Juryman 1 Ah.

Mother When they came and took her, I tried to explain. It was not her I wished to punish –

Juryman 1 So you believe she is guiltless?

Mother I believe she has erred.

Juryman 1 Erred repeatedly, vigorously, for nigh on eight months of marriage?

Mother I . . .

Juryman 1 You cannot pick and choose, Mrs Mülhahn.
Either you condemn them both, or you condemn yourself.

Mother But . . .
She is my child.

Juryman 1 You cannot allow filial affection to cloud your moral judgement.

Mother I would not have her die.

My only wish was to protect her.
The world is full of strange and frightening things. I saw
that she was – changing and . . . I did not wish to lose her.

After all, if I am not a wife, a mother, then – what am I?

Tell them, Catharina. Tell them it was a mistake.

Catharina refuses to meet her gaze.

Judge You will not address the co-defendant.

Mother I have always maintained decorum. I – I am a good
person.

Am I not?

Finally, blazingly, Catharina returns her gaze.

I cannot speak on her behalf. Ask her what she knew.
All I know is I am innocent. Just don't harm me.

*The Spinster motions, as if to hurry the memory along.
There is a bright flash of light accompanied by a
churning sound, as time moves forward.*

*A new witness appears on the stand. It is the Girl from
Act One, Scene One.*

Judge State your name for the record.

Girl Babette, milord.

Judge Babette what?

Girl Just Babette.

Judge 'Just Babette'.
Very well. Proceed.

Juryman 2 drags himself out of his seat.

Juryman 2 Miss . . . Babette. You met the defendant Miss
Linck during her time as a soldier, is that right?

Girl Yes, milord. At a dance, milord.

Juryman 2 That sounds jolly.

Girl It was, milord. Verily, milord.

Juryman 2 Did you know the defendant well?

Girl Know, milord?
    In the biblical sense, milord, yes, milord.

Judge Madam, much to our shock, Beuerlain has not yet
    been honoured with a title, thus you may address him as
    'sir', not 'milord'.

Juryman 2 Did you notice anything . . . unusual about him?

Girl Yes, sir.

Juryman 2 And what was that?

Girl He was keen to give me pleasure, sir.

Juryman 2 Pleasure?

Girl He had this technique of using one hand to frot me
    while / with the other he –

Judge Please refrain from lasciviousness in my court, madam.

Girl He knew how to fuck, sir. Is that enough detail for ye?

The Judge lets his head fall on the lectern.
    Speechless, Juryman 2 sits. Juryman 1 takes over.

Juryman 1 So am I to understand that you were aware of
    the defendant's – nature, Miss Babette?

Girl Oh yes, sir.

Juryman 1 Do you not have a – moral quandary with such
    perversity?

Girl I am not one to judge, sir.
    As I see it, if he acts like a man he's a man, sir. If he acts
    like a monster, he's that.

Juryman 1 And what did you make of the defendant's character?

Girl I found it to be – unique, sir.

Juryman 1 Aha. Unique. In what sense?

Girl I have been with countless types, sir. Most of 'em seek to be loved. He sought to love. It is not easily forgot.

Juryman 1 May I ask, what profession is it that you work in, Miss Babette?

Girl The oldest profession, sir.
And proud. I have raised three toothless babes, with no husband to speak on.

Juryman 1 Permission to strike the witness's testimony from the record, your honour? Surely the court cannot stoop to accepting the testimony of bawds.

Judge Sustained.

*Before the Girl can protest, the Judge bangs his gavel.
Another flash of light and the same churning sound.
The Doctor from Act One, Scene Five is on the stand.*

Doctor Francken. Dr Francken.

Juryman 1 You are employed by the Hanoverian troops, is that right?

Doctor Yes.

Judge Francken? We served together under General Schönberg back in the day, did we not?

Doctor So we did, your honour.

Judge A fine battalion.

Doctor Very fine.

Judge Are you thirsty? Fetch this man a drink, clerk. And me, while you're at it.

The Spinster goes to fetch some wine.

Go on, Arnt.
Make it quick. I am sure the doctor has better things to do.

Juryman 1 Much obliged, your honour.
You were the doctor assigned to Miss Linck's regiment, is that right?

Doctor I was.

Juryman 1 And you had occasion to examine her, did you not?

Doctor I did not.

Juryman 1 You did not?

Doctor No. She left the regiment before I had the chance.

Juryman 1 Left?

Doctor Yes.

Juryman 1 Deserted?

Doctor I . . .

The Doctor shoots Anastasius a nervous look.

I am not in a position to say, sir. I am merely responsible for the health of the battalion.

The Spinster brings some wine for the Doctor and the Judge.

Juryman 1 I see.

Judge (*raising his glass*) To old Schonny Schönberg!

Doctor To Schönberg.

Judge Don't mind me, Arnt.

Juryman 1 Since the doctor appears to have no recollection of the defendant, perhaps we may call on his medical expertise instead.

85

It is one of the obligations of this court to establish what punishment should be meted out to these – girls.
Clerk . . .

The Spinster brings out a huge, dusty book and opens it.

Spinster As stated in Article 116 of the Criminal Code, the punishment for a woman lying with a woman is death by burning.
The punishment for a man lying with a man is death by the sword.
The punishment for a man lying with an animal is death by hanging, followed by burning.

Juryman 1 Naturally the defendant Miss Linck must be punished for her crimes, but the question remains, which?

Doctor I do not understand.

Juryman 1 Ought she to be beheaded or burnt?

Doctor I . . . It is not for me to say.

Juryman 1 Oh?

Juryman 2 struggles to his feet.

Juryman 2 Your honour . . .

Judge Beuerlain, you are awake. What a pleasant surprise.

Juryman 2 Of course I am, your honour, this is a court of law.
Is it not clear that the defendant should be sentenced to death by fire? She is, after all, female.

Doctor In that case, your honour, one could argue that there should be no punishment at all. What harm is there in a couple of girls indulging in a little – play? It is insignificant.

Juryman 1 Well, now –

Doctor Copulation cannot occur without male and female organs.

Judge I think you will find that such copulation can, and indeed does, occur among men of a certain persuasion.

Juryman 1 can't resist.

Juryman 1 Do you speak from experience, your honour?

Judge Well, I –

The Judge realises what he is saying and bangs his gavel.

Order. That is not – pertinent to the . . .
I am not the subject of this . . .
Strike that from the record, clerk.

What say you, Francken?

Doctor I would point out that the scriptures do not denounce women for committing an 'abomination' when they lie together. Only men.

Juryman 2 Leviticus eighteen, verse twenty-two.

Juryman 1 Beuerlain, you show off.

Juryman 2 Although that same chapter does also state that wearing 'a garment mingled of linen and wool' is an abomination. These rules are somewhat archaic –

Juryman 1 Alright, that's enough.

Doctor Without semen, no fleshly union can / occur –

Judge I cannot quite believe we are discussing semen in my court.

Juryman 1 Your honour, perhaps there was no semen, but there was a search for the extinction of the libido. That is sex.

Doctor I disagree. All we can determine is whether – unnatural acts occurred –

Juryman 1 Tell me, Doctor, have you ever frigged yourself?

Judge Slander!

Juryman 1 I am merely seeking to determine whether the doctor has engaged in 'unnatural acts' himself and thus is guilty of hypocrisy.

Doctor Have you?

Judge Order! This is an upstanding gentleman, with a fine military career behind him –

Juryman 1 So, your honour?

Judge He will not be held to the same standards as a pair of common wretches.

Juryman 1 I see.

In that case, no further questions your honour.

Judge Please, Dr Francken . . .

Doctor If I may, your honour, as a medical man I limit my investigations to the corporeal realm. With respect to the spirit I cannot speak. In the end it is god who will judge us, each and every one. We ought not to forget that.

Judge But in this court, I am god. Let us not forget that.

*A flash of light and that same churning sound.
The Soldier is on the stand.*

State your name and place of birth for the record.

Soldier Friedrich Karl Rosenstengel. Of Calbe.

Judge Rosenstengel. The name appropriated by the defendant?

Soldier That is correct, your honour.

Judge No relation?

Soldier None, I'm afraid.

Judge A military man?

Soldier A lieutenant, your honour. With the Hanoverian Musketeers.

Judge Very respectable.
Gentlemen.

Juryman 1 stands, looking a bit surly after his chastisement by the Judge.

Juryman 1 You served with – Corporal Linck, did you?

Soldier Correct, sir.

Juryman 1 Did you think her trustworthy?

Soldier The most trustworthy, sir.

Juryman 1 What does that mean?

Soldier Only that I would trust him with my life, sir. He was a good friend.
Bit of a rogue when the mood took him, but aren't we all.

Juryman 1 Are we?

So you would have borne witness to Miss Linck performing – duties?

Soldier Correct, sir.

Juryman 1 Of what sort?

Soldier All sorts. Sword fighting. Cleaning our muskets. Patrolling. Keeping the peace / if necessary –

Juryman 1 And you never noticed her . . . lacking in facility?

Soldier Facility, sir?

Juryman 1 Strength. Self-command. Bravery.

Soldier No, sir.
If anything, he exceeded most.

Juryman 1 You expect us to believe that the fact she was a woman never interfered with her performance in one of the most physically challenging roles in the Prussian Guard today?

Soldier I do, sir.

Juryman 1 I cannot countenance such absurdity –

Soldier I must confess, among the men, strength and bravery were not always our strongest suits.

Juryman 1 Still.

Did you see her with women, Lieutenant?

Soldier Yes, sir.

Juryman 1 Chasing them? Seducing them?

Soldier Only those who wished to be seduced.

Juryman 1 Did they know she was born female?

Soldier I presume they took him as they found him, sir.

Juryman 1 But in your estimation –

Soldier I was not in their minds, sir – nor their hearts –

Juryman 1 But the fact remains, she lied –

Soldier Perhaps he was doing his best to be truthful, under the circumstances.

Juryman 1 You insist on referring to the defendant as 'he'.

Soldier Perhaps it is you who insist.

Juryman 1 She was born Catharina Margaretha Linck, to an illegitimate mother, circa 1694, in Halle.

Soldier I did not know him then. I know only my friend. Anastasius.

Juryman 1 Are you in contempt of this court, young man? You do know that is an offence? Punishable by flogging?

Soldier I am telling the truth before god, sir.

Juryman 1 No further questions.

Judge Beuerlain?

Juryman 2 heaves himself up, wheezing.

Juryman 2 I . . . I should like to know something of the charge of desertion –

Juryman 1 Your honour, desertion is a secondary offence. The purpose of this trial / is to –

Judge I do not need to be apprised of the purpose of this trial, Arnt.
I will thank you to remain in your seat until it is your turn to speak.
Beuerlain?

Juryman 2 What say you of the defendant's desertion, Mr . . . ah . . . Mr . . .

Soldier Rosenstengel.

Juryman 2 (*gasps*) But that is the name of the defendant!

Judge Yes. It is the name the defendant stole in order to commit her crimes, Beuerlain, which is why we are here, not in the tavern, as we all might wish.

Juryman 2 Ah, yes, quite.

Do you deny that the defendant deserted her post, Mr Rosenstengel?

Soldier I cannot.
But it does not surprise me.
I had the sense he was looking for a home. Somewhere people might accept him for who he was. I only wish we could have given it to him. Before it was too late.

Another bright flash of light and Catharina is on the stand.

Judge Catharina Margaretha Rosenstengel, née Miss
Mülhahn, as we shall call you for the purposes of this trial.
You have undergone interrogation, is that correct?

Catharina (*barely audible*) Yes.

Judge 'Yes, your honour' is the correct appellation.

Catharina Yes, your honour.

Judge And you have been – physically examined, to
establish the status of your maidenhood?

Catharina can barely get the word out.

Catharina Yes.

Judge And still the truth has not been arrived at in your
case.
Gentlemen?
And make it swift. We would all like to get home before
nightfall.

The Judge refills his cup of wine.
Both Jurymen begin to rise.

Juryman 1 Miss Mülhahn –

Juryman 2 Your honour –

Judge One at a time please. (*Mostly to himself.*) Like
herding blind cats.

*Juryman 1 waves Juryman 2 ahead with exaggerated
politeness.*

Juryman 2 Miss Mülhahn. Did you or did you not know
the truth of your husband's identity?

Catharina I . . .

Anastasius looks at Catharina.

I . . . do not rightly know, sir.

Juryman 2 shrugs elaborately, then retakes his seat.

Judge Is that the extent of your cross-examination?

Juryman 2 The co-defendant states that she does not know, your honour. I do not see how she can be expected to reveal what she does not know.

The Judge gives a long, pained sigh.

Judge Arnt. For the love of all that is holy . . .

Juryman 1 stands.

Juryman 1 Miss Mülhahn, when did you first encounter the defendant?

Catharina He rode past my house.

Juryman 1 I was given to understand that you met in a cloth shop.

Catharina That was the first time we met. Not the first time I saw him.

Juryman 1 So you knew he was a soldier? A deserter?

Catharina Not at first.

Juryman 1 Aha. The first deception.

Catharina But later –

Juryman 1 Let us begin with 'at first'.
What did you make of him?

Catharina I was intrigued.

Juryman 1 That intrigue led to a wedding in the year 1720, fourteen days before Michaelmas, at St Paul's Church, Halberstadt. Is that correct?

Catharina Yes.

Juryman 1 How was the day?

Catharina Beautiful.

Juryman 1 How endearing.
What happened after the service?

Catharina We went back to my mother's for some refreshments.

Juryman 1 And then?

Catharina We spent the night together.

Juryman 1 In what manner?

Catharina I suppose you might call it – conjugally.

Juryman 1 There is no room for supposition here. Enlighten us, Miss Mülhahn, in what manner did you 'spend the night'?

Catharina We . . . embraced. In bed.

Juryman 1 Did you?
And was that fun?

Catharina Objection.

Juryman 1 You do not object. I object. His honour the judge objects. You / do not –

Catharina I do not see the purpose of these lurid questions.

Juryman 1 Oh, I do apologise. Their purpose is to save your life.

Did you enjoy – and indeed initiate – sexual relations with your so-called husband?

Catharina Yes.

Juryman 1 You were not 'raped'? If indeed a husband can do such a thing to his wife.

Catharina No.

Juryman 1 Did you notice anything strange about it?

Catharina Sex is rather strange, do you not think?

Juryman 1 Not the sex I have experienced.
If I may be so free, your honour –

The Judge, who is in the middle of slurping his wine, waves a tired hand.

The sex I have experienced has been . . . ordinary.

Catharina Perhaps you have been doing it wrong.

Anastasius cannot help but let out a snort.
Catharina looks over. They catch each other's eyes, briefly, for the first time.

Juryman 1 Is there something humorous about being on trial for your life, young lady?

Catharina No, sir.

Juryman 1 Well then I suggest you curtail these giddy demonstrations.
The arrogance of young women today, your honour.

The Judge makes an indistinct grumbling sound.

Do you believe in god, Miss Mülhahn?

Catharina I believe there is something greater than ourselves, sir.

Juryman 1 A politic answer.
I take it you were pure, then, when you met the defendant?

Catharina It depends what you describe as pure.

Juryman 1 For the purpose of this dialogue, let us call it – untouched. By your hand or another's.

Catharina Then, no.

Juryman 1 Did you not seek to defend your chastity?

Catharina My entire life is taken up with 'defending my chastity'.

Am I pure? How pure? Have I ever seemed impure?
Could someone looking at me think I was impure and
therefore treat me as such?
Apparently we women are just walking hymens with
arms and legs to you lot.

Judge (*slurring his words*) That's a bit much.

Catharina I am merely answering the question.

Juryman 1 So you were impure.
You had known a man.

Catharina I had – experimented.

Juryman 1 Goodness. I am sure the imagination of many a
layman present is wondering at the thought.

Catharina I cannot control the minds of others.

Juryman 1 But you can control yourself.

Catharina Can you blame me for being curious to feel what
it was beneath a man's breeches that was so . . . awesome
that we ladies must be shielded from it?
If you must know, I was deeply underwhelmed.

Juryman 1 I say –

Catharina I did not know what pleasure was until I met my
husband.

Juryman 1 So you perceived a difference?

Catharina Between pleasure and its absence? Why, yes.

Juryman 1 Then you confess?

Catharina To what?

Juryman 1 Collusion?

Catharina Well, I –

Juryman 1 You just confessed. The defendant could not
hide from someone as sexually rapacious as yourself –

Catharina The root of my crime is my rapaciousness?

Juryman 1 Is that a question or a statement?

Catharina It is simply what you believe to be true.

Juryman 1 What I believe is not on trial here.

Catharina Perhaps one day it will be.

Juryman 1 Come now, Catharina, you are wasting good men's time. Did you or did you not know that this man – was a woman?

Catharina He is not.

Juryman 1 Come now.

Catharina My husband is not a woman.
He is neither man nor woman.

Judge Stuff and nonsense.

Catharina And it is a great act of bravery to be oneself in a world where others insist on pretending.

Judge Miss Mülhahn –

Catharina It is you who are deceived. You who insist that blue is blue and red is red. What of – purple?

Juryman 1 A clear case of hysteria, your honour –

Judge Miss Mülhorn – hahn. This court is not concerned with the nuances of colour. Here there are only two shades. Black and white.

Catharina Well that is absurd.

Judge It is the law.
Either you were deceived, in which case you will live. Or you knew the truth, in which case you must die.

Catharina The truth will kill me?

Juryman 1 This is impertinence, your honour.

Catharina I do not see why anyone need die, when no crime has been committed.

Judge You are not here to express your opinions on the penal code. Your opinions are irrelevant.

Juryman 1 She lacks respect for your authority.

Catharina What authority?

Judge Enough!
I will not be insulted. This is my court. I am the one with the – hammer thingy –

Catharina Gavel.

Judge And as long as that is the case, I make the decisions.
One or both of you must die tomorrow.
Which is it to be?

Catharina looks at Anastasius.

Juryman 1 Eternity is a long time, Miss Mülhahn.

Catharina It is.

Juryman 1 They say death by fire is agony.
Make your choice wisely.

Do you or do you not deny your husband?

Catharina I . . .

Anastasius silently implores her to save her own life.

I do.

Judge Good. Then I pronounce you innocent.
Ish.

He bangs his gavel.

Catharina Your honour –

Judge Shush, shush. I'm getting bored now.
You are evidently a weak-minded person who let herself be seduced into depravity. You will be condemned to

98

three years in the spinning room of the penitentiary,
afterwards to be banished from Prussia.

*He bangs his gavel again. A flash of blinding light.
Catharina disappears.*
Anastasius is on the stand.

Miss Linck. You are charged with desertion, for which
the punishment is flogging. And sodomy, for which the
punishment is still to be determined.
How do you plead?

Anastasius . . .

Juryman 1 She will not speak, your honour. I am told she
has not spoken a word since she was brought in.

Judge She will not speak?

Do you not wish to plead guilty or innocent?

Anastasius shakes their head.

You have no defence to present? None whatsoever?

Anastasius shakes their head.

You will speak in answer to my questions.

Anastasius remains silent.

Insolence.

If the defendant refuses to plead her innocence, then
I pronounce her guilty.

He bangs his gavel.

Juryman 1 Ought we not to interrogate her, your honour?

Judge Can't interrogate a brick wall.
(*To Anastasius.*) What of your punishment? Are you
happy to simply – waltz into the fire, or onto the block,
as we deem fit?

Anastasius I only ask, your honour, to die as I have lived.

Judge Very well. Then you will die by the sword.

He bangs his gavel again.

Thank god that's over.
Now, gentlemen, who's for the tavern?

Cries of assent from the Jurymen. The court is dismantled and the characters bustle off in all directions, with no apparent concern for what's just happened.

The Spinster is left gazing at Anastasius for a beat.

Then they are led away.

2

The sound of a cell door slamming shut. Out of the darkness, two small cells are lit side by side. Anastasius sits in one, in chains. Catharina sits in the other, unchained.

Anastasius moves and their chains clink noisily.

Catharina Anastasius?
Is that you?

Answer me.

Perhaps you are gagged. Move your chains if you can hear me?

Why did you not fight?
I thought you would charm your way out of it. I thought you would use rhetoric. Philosophy. Locke.
Why did you not speak?

My mother. My imbecilic mother. I knew she was a nincompoop. I knew she was self-seeking. I knew she was pitiable. I did not know she had such spite. She has stolen my life as hers was stolen, as if to enact some kind of . . . self-sabotaging vengeance.

We will never speak to her again.
Or see her. We will . . .

Anastasius. Please speak.

Perhaps we can fight it.
Tell them we lived as sisters. Companions –

Anastasius No.

Catharina Anastasius? Is that you?

Anastasius I will not lie to give them peace.

Catharina What a relief it is to hear your voice.
Come, let us plot our appeal. There must be a way –

Anastasius There is none.

Catharina You cannot mean to simply – accept defeat?

Anastasius On the contrary. I am such a threat that they
must destroy me to be sure of their own existence. That
is how I know I have won.

Catharina Do you not wish to live?

Anastasius What is a life if lived according to false rules?

Catharina A facsimile.

Anastasius A sham.

Catharina But – what is a life if not lived at all?

Anastasius An injustice.
But it is their injustice. Not ours.

Catharina Damn you, Anastasius. Fight.
Spar with me –

Anastasius How can I fight when I am in chains?

Catharina With words.

Anastasius There are no words.
Tell a person they are wrong, and they will fight.

Tell a person they are evil. They will fight.
Tell a person they are worthless. They will fight you night and day.
But tell a person they do not exist . . . How do you fight that?

Catharina So you intend to just . . . surrender?

Anastasius Silence is not surrender.
To live a lie or die honest – that is a false choice. My silence is all they deserve.

Catharina I am a fool.
A coward.
I let them rile me.

Anastasius No.

Catharina I fought back on their nonsensical terms.
I betrayed you –

Anastasius You were magnificent.

I was very proud.

Did you not think that old juryman with the gout bore an uncanny resemblance to a basset hound?

Catharina That is what it was.
I was trying to place it all through Mother's testimony.

Anastasius It was the eyes.

Catharina The eyes, yes. And the jowls.

The judge was a sot.

Anastasius I could smell his belches from where I sat.

Catharina Cursèd irony of him sending me to the spinning room. I always bloody hated embroidery.

The shadow has gone from my wall.
The sun must have risen.

Anastasius Our last night is nearly ended.

Catharina And we cannot even touch.
That is true cruelty.

Anastasius. Can we not run?

Anastasius Where?

Catharina Somewhere we can be ourselves.

Anastasius Such a place does not exist.
Yet.

It did for a time, in our little garret. With no privy and
rats in the rafters.

Catharina 'Nothing is truer than happiness, and nothing is
happier and sweeter than truth.'

Anastasius We were true to ourselves, Catty.
And we were happy.
Many cannot say the same of their whole lives.

Catharina What of your life?

Anastasius It has been . . . epic.

Catharina You cannot die. It is not time. We have so much
left to do.

Anastasius Be brave, Catty. You always were.

Catharina It is you who makes me brave.

Anastasius It is not.

Catharina I want to die too. I want to die with you.

Anastasius I cannot let that happen.

Catharina Why should you die and I live?

Anastasius Because they are afraid.

Catharina I cannot go on without you.

Anastasius You must. That is your part of the bargain.
I need you to keep writing. They may burn it, but if you
keep on, a part may yet survive –

Catharina I cannot.

Anastasius You must.
Tell our story. For those who will come after. A different
version from the one that they will tell.
Do not let my death be in vain.

Catharina How . . .

How will I ever forgive myself?

Anastasius It will be hard.
It may take time.
But there will come a day when, at least for a moment,
you will let go of your shame.
Promise me, you will try.

And when you are alone, from time to time, think of me,
eh?

Catharina Anastasius . . .

*The sound of a prison door being unlocked and swinging
open.*

Don't go.
It cannot be time yet.

Anastasius I love you, Catty. I love you –

Anastasius's cell disappears.

Catharina Anastasius?
Anastasius?
Please don't go. Not yet. Don't go. It is not time yet. Our
time is still to come.
Anastasius? Please.

My love?

Somewhere, a prison door slams and all is black.

A blank stage. In the centre a block, lit by a cold, white light.

Anastasius is led on. An Executioner in a hood stands to one side of them, holding a sword. On the other side is a Priest.

Priest May you be forgiven. In the name of the father, the son, and the holy ghost.

> *He makes the sign of the cross over Anastasius. Then steps back.*

Do you have any final words?

Anastasius thinks for a moment.

Anastasius Only to my wife. Catharina.
Catty.

Thank you. For your jests. Your wit. Your wisdom. Your inedible veal scallop. A thousand quiet moments. It is these that weave the fabric of a life.

Forgive the pain that I have caused you. You asked for a coxcomb and you got one, I'm afraid.
My solace is in knowing that there was pleasure too. In this short life, turbulent with troubles, we are blessed if we can give a little pleasure. A little joy. What else is it all for, in the end?

As for the rest of you. I repent nothing. I do not believe I have committed an offence by my existence. I only wish I had lived it louder. That there might be some ineradicable record of it for those who come after me, who wish to know that they are not the first to strive. We have always existed. We will always exist. Whether people accept us or no, it makes no odds. It merely determines how much we are made to suffer.

For, truly, it is my belief that even if I am to be done away with, those who are like me will remain.

Anastasius kneels.

The Executioner puts a black hood over their head.

They lean forward over the block.

The Executioner raises the sword.

As it comes down:

Utter darkness.

Act Five

Spinster Anastasius?

The Spinster is left standing alone, staring into the darkness.

There it is. The 'truth'.

Anastasius Lagrantinus Linck died in Halberstadt, Prussia, in 1721.
He was convicted of sodomy and sentenced to death by the sword.
Catharina Margaretha Mülhahn was sentenced to three years in the penitentiary, then exiled from Prussia.
That is where we leave her.
Me.

Those facts, bare and immutable, will be all that is left of us. Our story has unspooled itself. There is no more thread to follow.

But what is the good of speaking the truth if one cannot change it?

The Spinster wrestles.
    Then comes to a decision.

Beware the person who tells you, 'This is a true story.'
Whose truth? Told where? And when? To whom?
The truth is not an object to be found. It must be made. Crafted. Sewn of divers threads. And if it can be made. Then it can be unmade. Unravelled.
A new truth can be made. A new story.

And it is I who must write it. There is no more time to lose.

The same shiver of cello music that we heard at the start of the play. The same gauzy mist of time . . .

How to begin anew?

Two theatre chairs, the same as the ones the audience are sitting on, appear in the middle of the stage.

It begins in the same way. With two strangers. Some years in the distant future.
The first time they see each other they are . . .

In a theatre. The room is crowded. The show is about to begin.

The two actors who played Anastasius and Catharina enter. But this time they are in modern dress. They exist now, in our time. They take their seats.

One is wearing a white T-shirt and jeans. One is wearing dungarees.
And by god, do they look fine.

The two actors exchange shy looks. And smile.

They do not know it yet but this is a moment that will change them both forever.
Their lives will meet and intertwine, weaving a story of great passion. There will be suffering and there will be beauty.

They settle in to watch the play.

But that is all I can tell you. The rest you must imagine for yourselves.

The lights fade on the couple.

Blackout.

The names LINCK & MÜLHAHN are inscribed on the back wall of the stage in huge letters.